The Story of a Special Day
Volume 199

July
17

The 198th day of the year (199th in leap years). There are 167 days remaining until the end of the year.

by Michael Dobson

Timespinner
Press

This book is (or will be) available in e-book form for Kindland other formats from your favorite online booksellers.

For more information about the series, about us, or about your special day, please email us at editor@timespinnerpress.com.

Look for other volumes in *The Story of a Special Day,* coming often. See www.timespinnerpress.com for details and for the most recent information.

Table of Contents

Cover: The Sleeping Beauty Castle at Disneyland. Disneyland opened July 17, 1955 — the **EVENT OF THE DAY**.

Quote of the Day

"I suppose my formula might be: dream, diversify and never miss an angle."

Walt Disney
Disneyland opened July 17, 1955

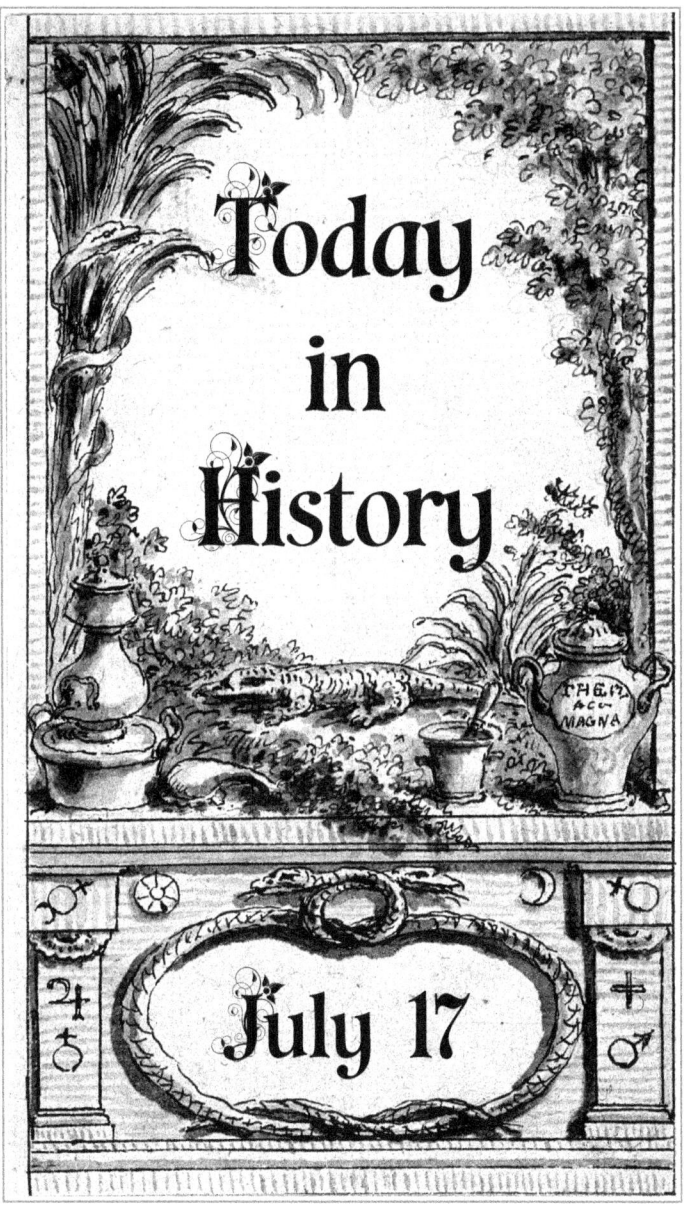

Today in History

July 17

Walt Disney

Event of the Day
July 17, 1955 — Disneyland Opens

On Sunday, July 17, 1955, in a special event broadcast live on ABC television, the Disneyland theme park opened. The only theme park designed and built by Walt Disney himself, Disneyland opened a new era in theme and amusement parks.

Disneyland today is the most visisted theme park in the world, with more than 650 million guests since its opening day, with over 16 million in 2013 alone! Popularly known as "the Happiest Place on Earth," it is far and away the best known theme park in the world.

Until the opening of Disneyland, Walt Disney was best known as an animator and film producer. In the 1920s, he founded Disney Brothers Studio with his brother Roy, and developed the iconic cartoon character Mickey Mouse in conjunction with his friend and fellow animator Ub Iwerks.

Although animation was historically confined to short films, Walt Disney pioneereed the development of full-length animated movies, beginning with 1937's *Snow White and the Seven Dwarfs,* the highest-grossing sound film at the time of its release. Other classic films followed, including *Pinocchio, Bambi,* and *Cinderella.*

The genesis of Disneyland came when Walt took his two daughters to Los Angeles's Griffith Park, one of the largest urban parks in North America.

Although most of the park is designed for hiking and other outdoor activities, a small number of concessions and attractions had been built.

While watching his daughters ride the merry-go-round, Walt came up with an idea for a park of his own. The popularity of his characters and films led to many requests to visit Disney Studios, but Walt realized that a functioning movie studio wouldn't have much of interest to a typical fan. Instead, he conceived something much greater.

The initial concept for what became Disneyland was detailed in a 1948 memo by Walt describing what was then called "Mickey Mouse Park." He originally planned for the park to be sited near his studio in Burbank, but quickly realized there was not enough space to create his dream. Instead, he acquired 160 acres in nearby Anaheim.

A park like Disneyland was unprecedented, and Walt had difficulty raising the necessary funds. He created a television show named *Disneyland* in partnership with ABC, and acquired other partners.as well. Construction of the park began on July 16, 1954, and opened one year and one day later. It cost $17 million, which is equivalent to about $180 million in 2016 dollars.

Although the opening celebration on July 17 was restricted to invited guests and media, nearly half the 28,000 attendees were either attending on counterfeit tickets or had snuck in by climbing over the fence.

Walt Disney shows Disneyland plans to local officials (Courtesy Orange County Archives, CC BY-SA 2.0)

The live television broadcast of the opening was anchored by TV host Art Linkletter, actor Bob Cummings, and actor (and future US President) Ronald Reagan.

Parts of the broadcast didn't go well. Guests were tripping over the television cables, Bob Cummings was caught kissing a dancer, and Art Linkletter lost his microphone. A local plumbers' strike forced Walt to choose between having working bathrooms or working drinking fountains. (He chose working bathrooms.) The large number of unexpected guests resulted in vendors running out of food. In later years, Disney executives would refer to opening day as "Black Sunday."

Public tickets went on sale the following day, with prospective guests showing up to get in line as early as two o'clock in the morning. Nearly 50,000 guests attended that first day.

Over the years, Disneyland has grown and changed. The original park opened with five "lands:" Main Street USA, Adventureland, Frontierland, Fantasyland, and Tomorrowland, and later added such attractions as New Orleans Square, Bear (later Critter) Country, and Mickey's Toontown.

Disneyland was successful beyond the wildest dreams of its creators, so much so that there was little room to expand. In 1971, the Disney organization opened Walt Disney World in Florida, and in the 1990s revamped Disneyland itself to add new shopping, new hotels, and a second park, Disney's California Adventure.

Walt Disney's vision continues to live. "To all who come to this happy place," Walt Disney said in his dedicatory remarks on July 17, "Welcome. Disneyland is your land. Here age relives fond memories of the past, and here youth may savor the challenge and promise of the future. Disneyland is dedicated to the ideals, the dreams, and the hard facts that have created America, with the hope that it will be a source of joy and inspiration to all the world."

Aerial view of Disneyland in 1962
(Courtesy Orange County Archives)

A locomotive on the Disneyland Railroad. Walt Disney was a
particular fan of railroads, and insisted one be part of his park.
(Credit: Tom Arthur, CC BY-SA 2.0)

The family of the last Tsar of Russia, Nicholas II. From left to right:
daughters Olga and Maria, Tsar Nicholas II and his wife Alexandra,
daughter Anastasia, son Alexei, and daughter Tatiana. All were
executed by Bolshevik troops on July 17, 1918.
(Courtesy Hermitage Museum)

What Happened on July 17?

From the creation of great works of engineering and art, to devastating wars and natural disasters, thousands of years of history have left their mark on each and every day of the year. Here are some important events that occurred on July 17. (Illustrated items are boxed.)

1717 — King George I of Great Britain sails down the River Thames on a barge with 50 musicians performing the world premiere of George Frideric **Handel's** *Water Music.*

Georg Friedrich Handel (left, with arm extended) and King George I of Great Britain (seated on chair) traveling down the Thames River on a barge while musicians play Handel's *Water Music* in the background. (Artist: Edouard Jean Conrad Hamman)

1762[*] — On the assassination of her husband Peter III, **Catherine the Great** (Екатерина II Великая) comes to power as empress regent of Russia.

1902 — The **first working air conditioner**, built by American inventor Willis Carrier, begins operating.

1917 — In response to anti-German sentiment during World War I, British monarch George V declares that the royal family would henceforth be known as the **House of Windsor**, instead of the House of Saxe-Coberg and Gotha. (His cousin, Kaiser Wilhelm II of Germany, remarked in response that he looked forward to seeing a production of *The Merry Wives of Saxe-Coberg Gotha*, a pun on Shakespeares *The Merry Wives of Windsor*.)

1918 — During the Russian Revolution, Bolshevik troops **execute the Imperial Romanov family** of Tsar Nicholas II. *(Photo pg. 12.)*

1936 — An attemped military coup against a recently elected Spanish government begins the **Spanish Civil War**, which will last two years and kill an estimated 500,000 people.

---

[*] Because Russia changed from the Julian calendar to the Gregorian calendar later than the rest of Europe, this date is equivalent to "O.S." (Old Style) July 6. See "What Day of the Week is July 17?" for more on different calendar types.

1938 — American aviator Douglas Corrigan files a flight plan from New York to Long Beach, California, and instead makes an unauthorized flight to Ireland after being refused official permission. Claiming he misread his compass and just went the wrong way, he earned the nickname **"Wrong Way" Corrigan.**

1945 — Winston Churchill, Joseph Stalin, and Harry S. Truman begin the **Potsdam Conference** to decide the fate of postwar Germany.

(from left to right) Churchill, Truman, and Stalin at Potsdam
(Courtesy Harry S. Truman Library)

1975 — In the **Apollo-Soyuz Test Project,** an American Apollo command module docks with the Soviet Soyuz 19 spacecraft in a major symbol of the policy of détente between the superpowers.

1984 — The **legal drinking age** in the United States is raised from 18 to 21.

1989 — The **first stealth bomber,** the Northrop Grumman B-2 Sprit, makes its first flight.

1998 — The **International Criminal Court** is established.

The B-2 Spirit gets ready for its first flight (Photo: MSGT Patrick Nugent, courtesy USAF)

Artist rendering of the Apollo-Soyuz Test Project (Courtesy NASA)

Quote of the Day

"I'm always making a comeback but nobody ever tells me where I've been."

Billie Holiday, singer
died July 17, 1959

Births
and
Deaths

July 17

Billie Holiday (Photo: William P. Gottlieb), who died July 17, 1959.

Notable July 17 People

With the current world population at about seven billion people, on average about 19 million people also celebrate their birthdays on July 17 — and that isn't counting the millions and millions who came before! No matter when you were born, you share your birthday with many special people whose accomplishments (and occasionally embarrassments) have been noted as part of history.

In this section, you'll meet fascinating people who share your birthday. They're organized by what they're famous for, and then in reverse chronological order from most recent to earliest. Those who are shown in photographs or artwork have a box around them. We don't have photos of everyone, so please forgive us if your favorite person is missing.

Some of these people you've heard of, others may be new to you, but they all make up an important part of the reason that July 17 is a truly special day!

John Jacob Astor, by John Wesley Jarvis
(Courtesy National Portrait Gallery)

Who Was Born on July 17?

Art and Photography

Quino, Argentine cartoonist known for his comic strip *Mafalda*, which ran throughout Latin America and Europe. *(1932)*

Arthur Rothstein, American photojournalist particularly known for his images of struggling rural farmers during the Great Depression. *(1915)*

Business and Technology

John Cooper, British car manufacturer who designed Formula One cars as well as the Mini Cooper. *(1923)*

Ephraim Shay, inventor of the Shay locomotive, which became the dominant locomotive of the steam rail era. *(1839)*

John Jacob Astor, first American multi-millionaire, his initial fortune came from fur trading but later expanded to real estate and opium. *(1763)*

Government and Politics

Angela Merkel, first female chancellor of Germany, often described as the de facto leader of the European Union, named "most powerful woman in the world" by *Forbes* magazine a record ten times. *(1954)*

Camilla, Duchess of Cornwall, second wife of Charles, Prince of Wales, heir apparant to the British throne. *(1947)*

Elbridge Gerry, 5th vice-president of the United States, namesake of "gerrymandering," the process of drawing political district lines to favor one party over another. *(1744 [O.S. July 6†])*

Journalism and Literature

Cory Doctorow, blogger, journalist, and science fiction writer, co-editor of the blog *BoingBoing,* activist in such areas as copyright liberalization. *(1971)*

J. Michael Straczynski, screen and comics writer who created the TV series *Babylon 5* and co-wrote such films as *Thor* and *World War Z. (1954)*

Mark Bowden, journalist whose best-selling book *Black Hawk Down* was made into a major motion picture. *(1951)*

LaVyrle Spencer, romance novelist with twelve New York Times bestsellers (several adapted into made-for-television movies), inducted into the Romance Writers of America Hall of fame. *(1943)*

---

† O.S. refers to the fact that different nations switched from the "old style" Julian calendar to the "new style" Gregorian calendar at different times. Gerry was born July 17 according to the Gregorian calendar, which corresponds to the old style date July 6. For more on calendar types, see "What Day of the Week is July 17?"

"The Gerry-Mander," an 1813 political cartoon by Elkanah Tisdale that first used the term.

Erle Stanley Gardner, attorney and novelist best known as the creator of Perry Mason. *(1889)*

Shmuel Yosef Agnon (שמואל יוסף עגנון), writer of Hebrew fiction who shared the 1966 Nobel Prize in Literature *(1888)*

Music

Luke Bryan, country music singer-songwriter whose hits include "I Don't Want This Night to End," "Drunk on You," and "Kiss Tomorrow Goodbye." *(1976)*

Regina Belle, singer-songwriter whose hits include "Baby Come to Me," "Make It Like It Was," and (with Peabo Bryson) "A Whole New World, the theme song to the Disney animated film *Aladdin.* *(1963)*

Nicolette Larson, American pop and country singer whose hits include "Lotta Love" and "That's How You Know When Love's Right." *(1952)*

Phoebe Snow, singer-songwriter best known for her 1975 hit "Poetry Man." *(1950)*

Ron Asheton, rock guitarist who co-founded The Stooges with Iggy Pop. *(1948)*

Spencer Davis, founder of the 1960s rock band The Spencer Davis Group. *(1939)*

Peter Schickele, composer and parodist best known for his musical comedy albums purportedly composed by the imaginary "P. D. Q. Bach," inventor of such musical instruments as the dill piccolo (for playing sour notes) and the tuba mirum (a tube filled with wine). *(1935)*

Vince Guaraldi, jazz pianist and composer particularly known for composing the music for the animated *Peanuts* specials. *(1928)*

George Barnes, swing jazz guitarist who made the first commercial recording of an electric guitar. *(1921)*

Performing Arts

Alex Winter, actor best known for playing Bill in the 1989 film *Bill & Ted's Excellent Adventure. (1965)*

David Hasselhoff, starred in the American television series *Knight Rider* and *Baywatch,* later developed a successful European music career, set Guinness World Records as the most watched man on television and having achieved the highest reverse bungee jump. *(1952)*

Lucie Arnaz, daughter of Lucille Ball and Desi Arnaz, appeared on numerous television series including her mother's *The Lucy Show* and *Here's Lucy,* as well as in her own eponymous series *The Lucie Arnaz Show. (1951)*

Tim Brooke-Taylor, comic actor known to British audiences for *I'm Sorry, I'll Read That Again* and *The Goodies. (1940)*

Donald Sutherland, actor whose many famous films include *The Dirty Dozen, M*A*S*H, Kelly's Heroes, Klute,* and *Don't Look Now;* father of actor Kiefer Sutherland. *(1935)*

Diahann Carroll, African-American actress and singer who appeared in some of the earliest major studio films to feature black casts (including *Carmen Jones* and *Porgy and Bess*); star of *Julia,* the first series on American television to feature a black woman in a nonstereotypical role; also known for her role on the primetime soap opera *Dynasty. (1935)*

Phyllis Diller, pioneering female stand-up comedienne and actress, known for her self-deprecating humor and exaggerated laugh; appeared in over 40 films and her own television series. *(1917)*

Art Linkletter, host of the long-running radio and television programs *House Party* and *People Are Funny,* authored a number of collection of quotes by children called *Kids Say the Darndest Things. (1912)*

Barbara O'Neil, actress who played Scarlett O'Hara's mother in *Gone With the Wind* and who received an Academy Award nomination for the 1940 film *All This, and Heaven Too. (1910)*

James Cagney, actor and dancer best known for his "tough guy" roles in such films as 1931's *The Public Enemy* and 1938's *Angels With Dirty Faces,* as well as for his Oscar-winning portrayal of George M. Cohan in the 1942 film *Yankee Doodle Dandy. (1899)*

James Cagney

Science

Gordon Gould, widely considered the inventor of the laser, known for his successful 30-year battle with the US Patent and Trademark Office over patent rights to the device; elected to the National Inventors Hall of Fame. *(1920)*

Georges Lemaître, priest and astronomer who developed the theory of the expansion of the universe and several scientific principles mistakenly credited to Edwin Hubble, including Hubble's Law and the Hubble constant; also first proposed what became known as the "Big Bang" theory of the origin of the universe. *(1894)*

Sports

Connie Hawkins, basketball player known as "The Hawk," member of the Naismith Memorial Basketball Hall of Fame. *(1942)*

Toni Stone, first woman to play professional baseball in the Negro Leagues, member of the International Women's Sports Hall of Fame. *(1921)*

Lou Boudreau, shortstop and later manager of the Cleveland Indians, holder of the MLB record for most consecutive doubles in a game, member of the National Baseball Hall of Fame. *(1917)*

Jack Laviolette, ice hockey player and manager who founded the Montreal Canadiens, the first team made up of French Canadian player; member of the Hockey Hall of Fame. *(1879)*

Connie Hawkins (Courtesy *The Sporting News* Archives)

The Assassination of Marat by Charlotte Corday, by Paul-Jacques-Aimé Baudry (Courtesy Musée des Beaux-Arts de Nantes)

Who Died on July 17?

Business and Economics

Katherine Graham, publisher of the Washington *Post* and daughter of Eugene Meyer. *(2001)*

Eugene Meyer, chairman of the Federal Reserve, first president of the World Bank, publisher of the Washington *Post* newspaper, father of Katherine Graham. *(1959)*

Adam Smith, moral philosopher and pioneering political economist famous for his highly influential 1776 work *The Wealth of Nations*. *(1790)*

Government and Politics

Charles Gray, 2nd Earl Grey, prime minister of the United Kingdom whose accomplishments include the abolition of slavery in the British Empire; Earl Gray tea is named for him. *(1845)*

Charlotte Corday, known as the "Angel of Assassination," executed by guillotine during the French Revolution for assassinating Jacobin leader Jean-Paul Marat in his bathtub. *(1793)*

Peter III of Russia (Пётр III Фёдорович), tsar of Russia for six months before being deposed and possibly assassinated, husband of Catherine the Great. *(1704 [O.S. July 6]‡)*

Journalism and Literature

Walter Cronkite, broadcast journalist who anchored the *CBS Evening News* for 19 years, named "the most trusted man in America" in a widely-quoted opinion poll; known for his show-ending catchphrase, "And that's the way it is." *(2009)*

Mickey Spillane, author of best-selling hard-boiled detective novels, including *I, the Jury* and *My Gun is Quick*. *(2006)*

Military and Exploration

Jim Bridger, famous mountain man and trapper in the western United States, discoverer of the Bridger Trail and Bridger's Pass, first European American to see the Great Salt Lake and one of the first to visit Yellowstone. *(1881)*

---

‡ See "What Happened on July 17?" for more on Catherine the Great. "O.S." stands for "Old Style," because Russia converted from the Julian to the Gregorian calendar later than the rest of Europe. July 17 in "old style" reckoning is the same as July 6. For more on calendar types, see "What Day of the Week is July 17?"

Mickey Spillane

Jim Bridger

Pierre-Charles Le Sueur, French fur trader and explorer, first known European to explore the Minnesota River valley, namesake of the Le Sueur line of frozen and canned vegetables. *(1704)*

Music

John Coltrane, influential jazz saxophonist in bebop, hard bop, and free jazz, also noted for his spirituality; received a special Pulitzer Prize in 2007 and was canonized by the African Orthodox Church. *(1967)*

Billie Holiday, influential jazz singer-songwriter, subject of the 1972 biopic *Lady Sings the Blues*, major hits include "Strange Fruit," "I've Got My Love to Keep Me Warm," and "God Bless the Child." *(1959)* *(Photo pg. 20)*

Performing Arts

Elaine Stritch, actress who earned four Tony nominations for Broadway roles, best known to television audiences as the mother of network chief Jack Donaghy on the sitcom *30 Rock. (2014)*

Geraldine Fitzgerald, actress nominated for an Oscar for her role in the 1939 film *Wuthering Heights,* also known for roles in *Dark Victory* (1939) and *Arthur* (1981), member of the American Theater Hall of Fame. *(2005)*

Science and Medicine

William James Sidis, child prodegy claimed to have the highest IQ ever recorded, entered Harvard University at the age of eleven, and received his degree at the age of sixteen. Committed to a sanitarium to "reform" him after serving 18 months for participating in a political rally, Sidis spent the remainder of his life working menial jobs and obsessively collecting streetcar transfers. *(1944)*

Henri Poincaré, mathematician, physicist, and philosopher whose contributions include the famous Poincaré conjecture and the creation of a new branch of mathematics; provided important foundation work that led to Einstein's Theory of Relativity. *(1912)*

Dorothea Dix, activist for the mentally ill who lobbied for the creation of the first generation of American mental asylums, served as Superintendent of Army Nurses during the American Civil War. *(1887)*

Sports

Dizzy Dean, pitcher for the St. Louis Cardinals, Chicago Cubs, and St. Louis Browns; became a popular sports commentator following his playing career; member of the National Baseball Hall of Fame.

Ty Cobb, outfielder for 22 seasons with the Detroit Tigers, widely considered one of the greatest baseball players of all time, with multiple records including highest career batting average (.367); received the most votes of any player to be part of the inaugural class of the Baseball Hall of Fame. *(1961)*

Ty Cobb (Courtesy New York *Times*)

July, by Eugène Grasset

Quote of the Day

"Hatred and anger are the greatest poison to the happiness of a good mind."

Adam Smith, economist and philosopher
died July 17, 1790

Holidays
Around
the World

July 17

Poster for the 140th National Flag Day, 1917. **National Flag Week** is celebrated each year during the week that includes July 14.

Holidays Around the World

If you're looking for a reason to take your special day off, you should know that every single day is a holiday somewhere in the world! Here's some of what you can celebrate on July 17!

Fixed Celebrations

- **Constitution Day (**제헌절**)** (South Korea)

- **Independence Day (Výročie deklarácie o zvrchovanosti SR)** (Slovakia)

- **International Firgun Day** (international, derived from the modern Hebrew word *firgun* (פירגון), which describes generosity of spirit, empathic joy, and unselfish delight in the accomplishments of others.)

- **King Letsie III's Birthday** (Lesotho)

- **U Tirot Sing Day** (Meghalaya India, commemorating Khasi chief U Tirot Sing, who fought against British attempts to take control of the Khasi Hills)

- **World Day for International Justice** (international)

Moveable and Multi-Day Events

Some events take place over a specific week or time period. Start and finish dates may vary from year to year. Some events occur on different days each year (such as "fourth Saturday" of a given month). These events sometimes take place on July 17.

Week containing National Flag Day (July 14)

- National Flag Week (US) *(Photo pg. 42)*

Second Saturday in July

- International Young Eagles Day
- Missing Mutts Awareness Day
- World Bike Naked Day

Second Sunday in July

- Abused Women and Children's Awareness Day
- Children's Sunday
- Multicultural American Child Day
- Race Unity Day

Religious Feast Days and Holidays

Every religion normally has feast days and holidays associated with it. While some religious days take place on a given calendar day, others occur on different days each year, usually because the date is determined by the phases of the Moon rather than the Earth's path around the Sun. Here are some religious feasts, festivals, and holidays that sometimes or always fall on July 17.

Observances

Month of the Most Precious Blood of Jesus
(Catholicism)

Saint Days

Each day in the year is considered a feast day for one or more saints. They are somewhat different in western Christianity (Catholicism and many forms of Protestantism) and in eastern (Orthodox) Christianity.

In **Western Christianity,** July 17 is the feast day of Saints Alexius of Rome, Cynehelm, Cynllo, Magnus Felix Ennodius Marcellina, Piatus of Tornai, Pavel Peter Gojdič (Greek Catholic Church) and William White (Episcopal Church).

In **Eastern Orthodox Christianity,** it is also the commemoration of Saints Leonides of Ustnedumsk, Euphrasius of Ionopolis, and the Russian Imperial Family (Russian Orthodox Church). (These saints are honored on July 30 by Old Calendrists.[§])

In **Coptic Orthodox Christianity,** which uses its own calendar, July 17 is the equivalent of the 23rd day of the month of Epip. They commemorate St. Longinus the Soldier and St. Marina of Antioch.

[§] "Old Calendrists" use the Julian, rather than the Gregorian, calendar. For an explanation of different calendar types, see "What Day of the Week is June 18?"

Celebrations About Food

In the United States, almost every day of the year is dedicated to a particular food. (Some other countries also have official food days, but only in America is there one every single day!) Sponsored by manufacturers, retailers, farmers, or simply fans, these days are often proclaimed by the President, Congress, state governors, or mayors. Given that there are more different foods than days of the year, some days honor more than one kind of food!

Some foods just get a day, while others get a whole month. Here's what to eat on July 17 and the rest of the month of July!

July 17 is **National Peach Ice Cream Day.** It's also **National Ice Cream Month**, so try a different flavor each day. According to Foodimentary, Americans eat more ice cream than any other country — an astounding 48 pints per person per year!

Various sources list the following foods promoted during the month of July...

- National Baked Beans Month
- National Blueberry Month
- National Candy Month
- National Culinary Arts Month
- National Fruit and Veggies Month
- National Grilling Month

- National Honey Month
- National Hot Dog Month
- National Pickle Month
- National Picnic Month
- National Rosé Wine Month
- National Watermelon Month

A Ford Model A ice cream van at the Henry Ford Museum (Photo: Alf van Beem) — for **National Ice Cream Month**

Honorary Months

Presidents, Congresses, and nations around the world issue proclamations recognizing particular months to honor certain causes. These events generally fall in April, though honorary months do come and go.

Holidays established by states and nonprofit organizations are listed if verified. If not otherwise specified, all months are US. There is some variation from year to year; some celebratory months get added and others get dropped. Two places to get up to date information are the current edition of Chase's Calendar of Events *or the website Brownielocks. Here are some honorary designations for July.*

Health

- Bereaved Parents Awareness Month
- Fragile X Awareness Month
- Group B Strep Awareness Month (US, UK)
- Herbal/Prescription Interaction Awareness Month
- Juvenile Arthritis Awareness Month
- National Wheelchair Beautification Month

Recreation

- Family Golf Month
- National Park and Recreation Month
- National Vacation Rental Month
- Women's Motorcycle Month

Society

- Cell Phone Courtesy Month
- Get Ready for Kindergarten Month
- National Black Family Month

Just for Fun

Anybody can make up a holiday, and many people do. While none of these are officially recognized and some may come and go, here are a few more holidays for July 17.

- National Get Out of the Doghouse Day

- World Emoji Day
- Yellow Pig Day (celebrated by mathematicians in honor of the number 17)

Dog in Doghouse with Frog, by Clara von Willie
for **National Get Out of the Doghouse Day**

Quote of the Day

"The English winter — ending in July,
To recommence in August."

— Lord Byron, *Don Juan*

About the Month of July

July, from the *Brevarium Grimani* by Simon Bening (c.1510)

July: The Seventh Month

> *"Hot July brings cooling showers,*
> *Apricots and gillyflowers."*
> — *Sara Coleridge, "The Months".*

In the original Roman calendar, the month of July was named *Quintilis*, the fifth month, because the Romans originally counted the first of March as the beginning of the new year.

Quintilis was renamed July by the Roman senate in honor of Gaius Julius Caesar after his death in 44 BCE, because Caesar, among his other accomplishments, had undertaken a major calendar reform, known as the Julian calendar, which remained the standard European calendar until 1582 CE. (Not to be outdone, Emperor Augustus arranged for the next month, Sextilis, to be renamed in his honor.)

July is one of the seven months with 31 days. In a common (non-leap) year, it always starts on the same day of the week as April, and on the same day of the week as January in leap years. Strangely, in common years, no other month of the year ends on the same day of the week as July! (In leap years, the last day of July and January fall on the same day.)

July in Other Cultures

In Latin, the month of July was spelled *Iulius*, as the Romans did not have the letter "J."

In Albanian, the month is *korrik*. Arabs call the month يوليه (*yūlia*).

It is юли (*juli*) in Bulgaria, *lipanj* in Croatia, and *červen* in Czech.

The Finns call the month *kesäkuu* and the Greeks call it Ιούλιος (*Ioúlios*).

The Hebrew calendar has different months, but when they refer to the Gregorian month, it's יולי (*yûlî*).

In Gaelic, July is *Meitheamh mi an Mheitheamh*, and in Russian, it is июнь (*ijun'*).

The Chinese use 六月 (*liùyuè* in Mandarin); Koreans 유월 (*yuweol*); and it's 腸趏 (*tháng sáu*) in Vietnamese.

July Sayings and Superstitions

Farming

- The corn harvest will be good if the corn growing in the fields is "knee high by the Fourth of July."
- "If the first of July be rainy weather, 'twill rain more or less for four weeks together."
- "Rain or dry, plant your turnips on the Fourth of July."

- A swarm of bees in May is worth a load of hay. A swarm of bees in June is worth a silver spoon. A swarm of bees in July is not worth a fly.

Marriage

- "Those who in July do wed, must labor for their daily bread."

As for which day of the week, that's easy.

Monday for health, Tuesday for wealth,
Wednesday best of all, Thursday for losses,
Friday for crosses, Saturday for no luck at all.

July Symbols

Birthstone: Ruby (symbolizes success, devotion, and integrity.)

According to an old English proverb, "The glowing Ruby should adorn / Those who in warm July are born, / Then will they be exempt and free / From love's doubt and anxiety."

Ruby

Birth Flowers: Water Lily (purity of heart) or Larkspur (lightness and levity.)

Water Lily (Photo: Dinkum)

Birth Tree: Elm (strength of will and intuition)

"Study of an Elm Tree," John Constable (1821)

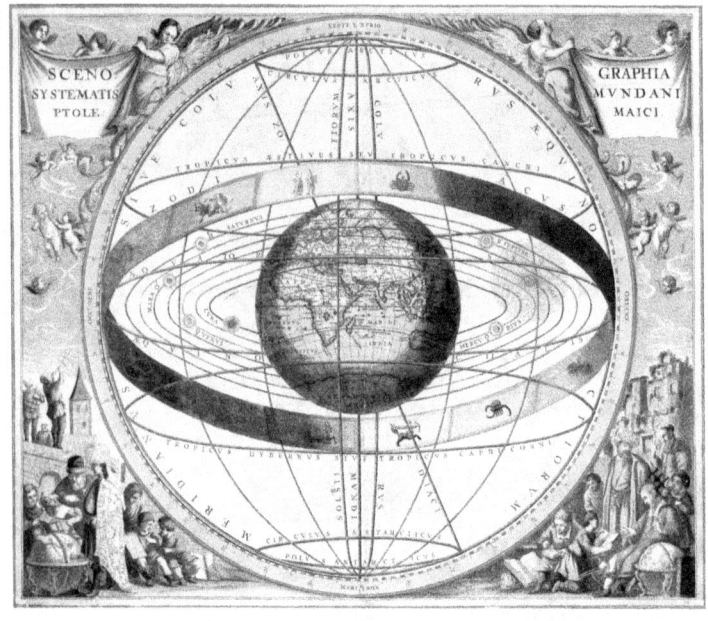

Scenography of the Ptolemaic Cosmography, by Johannes van Loon, based on Andreas Cellarius's *Harmonia Macrocosmica*, 1660

July 17 Zodiac Signs

From the perspective of someone on Earth, the Sun appears to move through the sky throughout the year, along a path astronomers call the *ecliptic plane*. The ecliptic plane is divided into twelve constellations, known as the zodiac, based on traditionally observed patterns of stars. On your birthday, you can't see your constellation, because it's in the daytime sky.

The zodiac was first developed by Babylonian astronomers about 2,500 years ago. Because they were unaware that the Earth wobbles like a spinning top (known as *precession*), they didn't make allowance for the fact that the Sun's path through the zodiac changes over time.

That means there are now two sets of dates for your birth sign. The *tropical dates* are the original Babylonian dates; the *sidereal dates* tell you where the Sun actually appears as it moves along its annual path.

July 17, however, is one of the few days each year in which the tropical and sidereal sign is the same: **Cancer.**

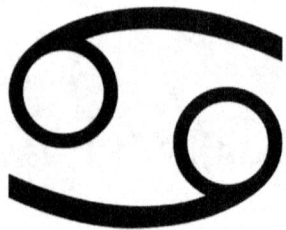

Cancer

Tropical June 21 to July 22
Sidereal July 16 to August 15

The Greek word for "crab" is Καρκινος (Karkinos), later Latinized as carcinus, which evolved into our word cancer. In Greek mythology. In one telling, when Hercules was battling the Hydra, Zeus's wife Hera sent Karkinos to distract the hero, but Hercules kicked it with such force that it was thrown into the sky, becoming a constellation. (Some say that Hercules crushed the crab with his foot and that Hera placed the crab in the night sky as a reward for its service.)

Because of the association with the disease, some astrologers refer to those born under the sign of Cancer as "moon children," because the ruling planet of Cancer is the Moon.

Cancers (or Moon Children) are supposed to be loyal, dependable, caring, and adaptable, but can also be moody, self-pitying, and oversensitive. Cancers are supposed to be particularly compatible with Scorpios, Piceans, and other Cancers.

The Sign of Cancer, by Giovanni Maria Falconetto (Courtesy Palazzo d'Arco, Mantua, Italy)

Illustration by Edward Penfield

What Day of the Week is July 17?

On what day of the week does July 17 fall?

Surprisingly, this isn't an easy question. Because the calendar year is 365 days long (366 in leap years), it doesn't divide evenly by the seven days of the week.

Also, the Earth goes around the Sun in about 365-1/4 days, so a calendar tends to drift over time. That's why the same date falls on different weekdays in different years.

This is made even more complicated by a change in calendars that took place in 1582. Our modern calendar has its roots in ancient Rome, in a calendar reform conducted by Julius Caesar. Caesar commissioned mathematicians to attack the problem, and they came up with the idea of leap years, and thus standardized the calendar for centuries to come. This was called the Julian calendar.

Over time, however, the small errors in Caesar's calculation compounded. That's why Pope Gregory XIII commissioned the Gregorian calendar, used in most of the world today. Some countries converted in 1582, when the calendar was first developed; some converted later; other still haven't changed.

Gregorian and Julian aren't the only types of calendars. The Hebrew year, the Islamic year, and many other calendars are used in different parts of the world and among different people.

You can convert Gregorian dates to other calendars, including the Hebrew calendar, the Islamic calendar, and even the Mayan calendar by visiting the Fourmilab Calendar Converter at http://www.fourmilab.ch/documents/calendar/.

Chinese calendar systems are quite complex and have changed several times; a full discussion is far beyond the scope of this book. If you're interested, you can find information here: http://www.hermetic.ch/cal_stud/chinese_cal.htm.

On Names and Dates

Historians use "CE" (Common Era) and "BCE" (Before the Common Era) instead of the more common "AD" (Anno Domini, or Year of Our Lord) and "BC" (Before Christ), reflecting the fact that the year-numbering system established by the Gregorian calendar is used throughout the world in many countries not culturally Christian.

The CE/BCE designation dates back to at least 1708, and has been adopted as a standard by the United Nations and the Universal Postal Union. Because this series of books covers events and people of all nations and cultures, we use the CE/BCE terms.

The abbreviation "O.S." ("Old Style") and "N.S." ("New Style") on some dates refers to the fact that the Russian Empire (in particular) did not switch from the Julian to the Gregorian calendar at the same time as the rest of Europe, and therefore some figures and events have two dates.

Also, in the Julian calendar in England in the 16th century, the year began on March 25 rather than January 1. To avoid confusion with Gregorian dates, dates between January and March were often written using both years.

People and events whose original names are not in the Western alphabet have their native names (where possible) in the appropriate script shown in parenthesis. If you are using an e-reader to access an electronic version of this book, all characters don't always display on all devices.

A 50-year brass perpetual calendar.

Quote of the Day

"Time is an illusion, lunchtime doubly so."

Douglas Adams,
from *The Hitchhiker's Guide to the Galaxy*

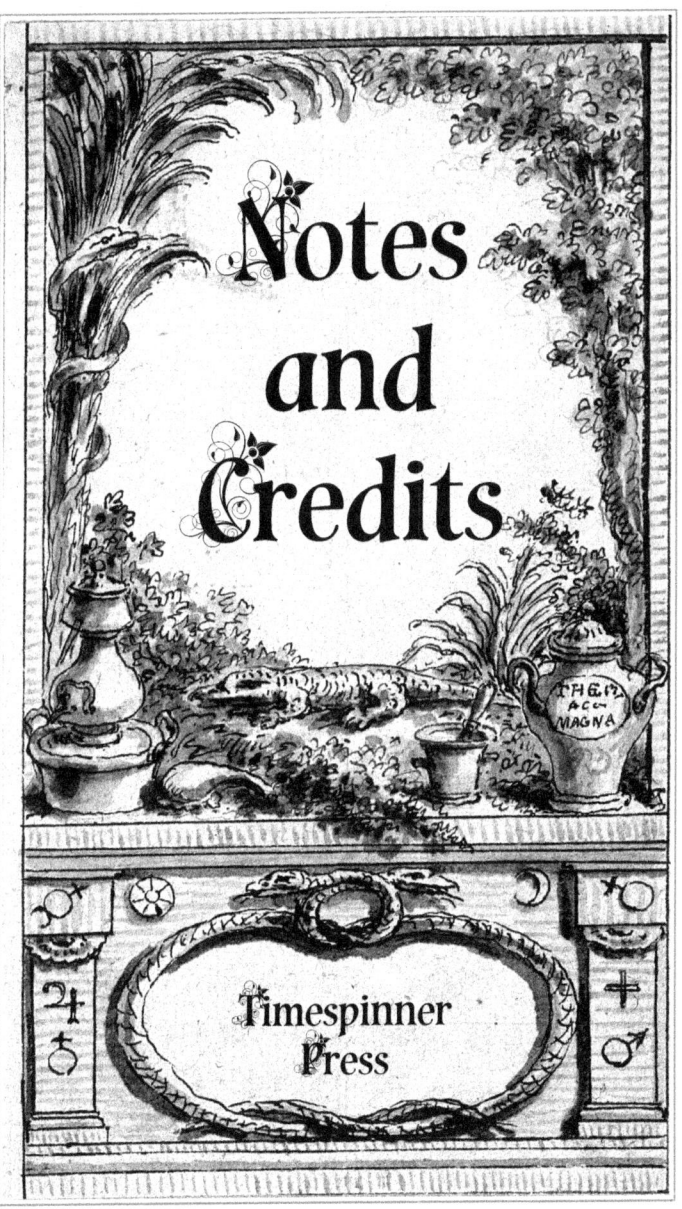

Notes and Credits

Timespinner
Press

Cartoon by John T. McCutcheon

Copyright, Credit, and Contact

Follow Us

Our blog "This Day in History" (http://
timespinnerpress.com/this-day-in-history/) features short
articles on events and people associated with each day, and
updates several times each week. Also subscribe to the
"Quote of the Day" at http://timespinnerpress.com/quote-
of-the-day/. You can get daily links by following us on
Facebook at TimespinnerPress, or on Twitter as
@sidewisethinker.

Contact Us

Find an error or a format problem? Want information about
the series, about us, or about when the volume for your
special day might be available? Please email us at
editor@timespinnerpress.com. (We also take requests if your
special day isn't yet complete. Please give us at least six
weeks' notice if possible.)

Sources

We owe a great debt to Wikipedia, which is our first stop for
research. We attempt to make independent confirmation of
all important dates and facts through a variety of other
sources.

Other sources we frequently use include the Library of
Congress; "on this day" listings from *Encyclopedia Britannica*,
the *New York Times*, and the BBC; Omniglot for the names of
months in other languages; *Chase's Calendar of Events*; and, of
course, the always essential Google.

All art and photographs are either in the public domain, used under a Creative Commons license, or with a "fair use" justification, and most frequently come from Wikimedia Commons and the Library of Congress Prints and Photographs Division.

Attribution is provided where possible, or as requested by the copyright owner, or when there is particular historical significance, listed below. For information about any particular illustration or photograph, please contact us.

Credits

1. The 2016 photograph of the Sleeping Beauty Castle at Disneyland was taken by "HarshLight," and is used here under CC BY-SA 2.0.

2. The illustration of the month of July used on the back cover is from the French Gothic illuminated manuscript *Les Très Riches Heures du duc de Berry* by the Limbourg Brothers, Jean Colombe, and an intermediate painter whose name is lost to history. It is in the public domain because its copyright has expired.

3. The box graphic used on the first page is from a 1916 pamphlet entitled "Divorce versus Democracy" authored by G. K. Chesterton, originally published in London by the Society of St. Peter and St. Paul. It is in the public domain in the US because it was published prior to 1923, and is in the public domain in all countries (including the country of origin) in which the copyright time is the author's life plus 70 years or less.

4. The graphic design for the section pages in this book is from a design originally created for a pharmacy label. It is courtesy of Wellcome Images (ICV No 11073, photo V0010813), and is used here under CC BY-SA 4.0.

5. The 1954 photograph of Walt Disney was cropped from a larger photo of Disney with Werner von Braun, and is in the public domain as a work created by an employee of NASA. It is courtesy Marshall Space Flight Center, photo ID GPN-2000-000060.

6. The 1954 photograph of Walt Disney showing Disneyland plans to Orange County officials is courtesy of the Orange County Archives, and is used here under CC BY-SA 2.0.

7. The 1962 aerial view photograph of Disneyland is from the Alfred B. Osterhues Collection (Ac2015.14), and is courtesy Orange County Archives. It is used here under CC BY-SA 2.0.

8. The 2009 photograph of the Disneyland steam locomotive "E. P. Ripley" was taken by Tom Arthur, and is used here under CC BY-SA 2.0.

9. The 19th century painting of Handel and King George on a barge during the first performance of Water Music is by Edouard Jean Conrad Hamman, and is in the public domain because its copyright has expired.

10. The 1913 portrait photograph of Tsar Nicholas II of Russia and his family is in the public domain in Russia according to article 1256 of Book IV of the Civil Code of the Russian Federation No. 230-FZ of December 18, 2006. It is in the public domain in the United States because it was first published prior to January 1, 1923. The photograph was taken by Levitsky Studio, Livadiya, and is from the collection of the Hermitage Museum, St. Petersburg, Russia.

11. The 1945 photograph from the Potsdam Conference is in the public domain as a work taken by an employee of the US government as part of that person's official duties. It is courtesy of the Harry S. Truman Library (NARA ARC Identifier 198958).

12. The photograph of a B-2 bomber at the Air Force Test Center was taken by Master Sergeant Patrick Nugent and is in the public domain as a work taken by a member of the US military as part of that person's official duties. It is courtesy USAF and from the defenseimagery.mil website, VIRIN DF-ST-90-07393.

13. The 1973 artist's rendering of the Apollo-Soyuz Test Project is in the public domain as a work created by NASA.

14. The photograph of Billie Holiday at the Downbeat jazz club was taken by William P. Gottlieb in 1947. It is part of the William P. Gottlieb collection donated to the Library of Congress (digital ID gottlieb.04211). All photographs in this

collection entered the public domain on February 16, 2010, in accordance with the wishes of William Gottlieb.

15. The painting of John Jacob Astor by John Wesley Jarvis was created circa 1825, and is in the public domain because its copyright has expired. The original is in the collection of the Smithsonian Institution's National Portrait Gallery (NPG. 78.204); the image is courtesy Google Art Project.

16. The cartoon "The Gerry-Mander" by Elkanah Tisdale is cropped from the front page of the Salem (Massachusetts) *Gazette*, Vol. XXVII, Issue 27, April 2, 1813. It is in the public domain because its copyright has expired. The image is courtesy of the Cornell University Library, accession number 1003.01.

17. The Warner Brothers publicity photo of James Cagney was taken sometime during the 1930s. It is in the public domain because it was first published in the United States between 1923 and 1977 without a copyright notice. Typically, publicity photographs are not copyrighted because of the way in which they are intended to be used.

18. The 1968 photograph of Connie Hawkins was taken sometime during the 1930s. It is in the public domain because it was first published in the United States between 1923 and 1977 without a copyright notice. The image is courtesy *The Sporting News* Archives.

19. The 1860 painting *L'Assassinat de Marat/Charlotte Corday* by Paul-Jacques-Aimé Baudry is courtesy Musée des Beaux-Arts de Nantes (accession number 802). It is in the public domain because its copyright has expired.

20. The 1974 publicity photo of Mickey Spillane is in the public domain because it was first published in the United States between 1923 and 1977 without a copyright notice. Typically, publicity photographs are not copyrighted because of the way in which they are intended to be used.

21. The photograph of Jim Bridger is courtesy of the Noah H. Rose Collection, Denver Public Library, call number Z-314. It is in the public domain because its copyright has expired.

22. The 1917 photograph of Ty Cobb was originally published in the New York Times and was copyright Bettman/Corbis. It

is in the public domain because it was first published prior to January 1, 1923.

23. The 1896 illustration of July is by Eugène Grasset. It is in the public domain because its copyright has expired.

24. The 1917 poster for the 140th Flag Day is in the public domain because its copyright has expired.

25. The photograph of a Ford Model A ice cream van was taken at the Henry Ford Museum by Alf van Beem, who released the image into the public domain.

26. The 1881 painting *Der Frosch (Hund in Hundehütte mit Frosch)* by Clara von Willie is in the public domain because its copyright has expired.

27. The painting "July" is from the *Brevarium Grimani,* circa 1510, and is in the public domain because its copyright has expired.

28. The photograph of a ruby was released into the public domain by its creator.

29. The photograph of a water lily at Kew Gardens was taken by "Dinkum," who released it into the public domain under the CC0 1.0 dedication.

30. The 1821 painting "Study of an Elm Tree" by John Constable is in the public domain because its copyright has expired. The painting is in the collection of the Victoria & Albert Museum, London.

31. The celestial sphere is from *Scenography of the Ptolemaic Cosmography,* by Johannes van Loon, based on Andreas Cellarius's *Harmonia Macrocosmica,* 1660. It is in the public domain because its copyright has expired.

32. The fresco "Sign of Cancer" by Giovanni Maria Falconetto was painted between 1515 and 1520, and is in the public domain because its copyright has expired. The image is courtesy Palazzo d'Arco, Mantua, Italy.

33. The 1906 automobile calendar is by Edward Penfield, and is in the collection of the Library of Congress Prints and Photographs Division. It is in the public domain because its copyright has expired.

34. The 50-year perpetual calendar photograph is in the public domain.

35. The cartoon by John T. McCutcheon is from his 1905 collection *The Mysterious Stranger and Other Cartoons* by John T. McCutcheon. It is in the public domain because its copyright has expired.

License Description and Terms

Aside from material purely in the public domain, photographs and other material in this book are used under specific licenses permitting free use, usually with an attribution requirement. For full text and terms of these licenses, click or enter the appropriate links below. If you believe there is an error in the copyright status or attribution of any of these images, please email us.

- Creative Commons Attribution 2.0 Generic (CC-BY 2.0): http://creativecommons.org/licenses/by/2.0/deed.en
- Creative Commons Attribution-Share Alike 3.0 Generic (CC-BY-SA 3.0): http://creativecommons.org/licenses/by-sa/3.0/
- Creative Commons Attribution-Share Alike 2.5 Generic (CC-BY-SA 2.5): http://creativecommons.org/licenses/by-sa/2.5/deed.en
- Creative Commons Attribution-Share Alike 2.0 Generic (CC-BY-SA 2.0): http://creativecommons.org/licenses/by/2.0/deed.en
- Creative Commons Attribution-Share Alike 1.0 Generic (CC-BY-SA 1.0): http://creativecommons.org/licenses/by-sa/1.0/deed.en
- CC0 1.0 Universal (CC0 1.0) Public Domain Dedication (CC0 1.0) http://creativecommons.org/publicdomain/zero/1.0/deed.en
- GNU Free Documentation License (GFDL): http://en.wikipedia.org/wiki/Wikipedia:Text_of_the_GNU_Free_Documentation_License
- License Art Libre (Free Art License): http://artlibre.org

Other Books from Timespinner Press

The Story of a Special Day
Michael Dobson

A series of (eventually) 366 volumes covering everything that happened on your special day! Events, births, deaths, quotes, holidays, and much more. It's like a birthday card they'll never throw away!

US$7.95 print / US$2.99 ebook.

From Plassey to Pakistan
Humayun Mirza

The history of British Colonial India and the formation of Pakistan from the unique perspective of the son of Pakistan's first president and last of the royal line of Bengal, Bihar, and Orissa! This unique historical document tells the inside story of this distinguished family, including the detailed story of the coup that toppled his father from power!

US$27.95 print

A Whole New Navy: America's War in the Pacific

Miles Durr

The most comprehensive and detailed description of America's naval war in the Pacific ever—every battle, every ship, every task force and every task group from Pearl Harbor through the Japanese surrender! A must-have for the collection of every World War II buff!

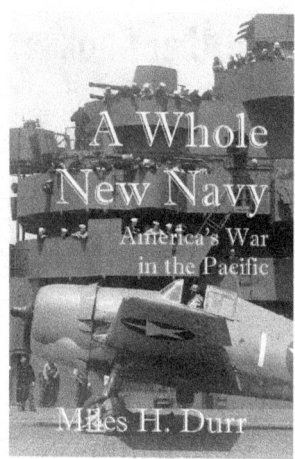

US$29.95 print

Improbable History: The Weird, the Obscure, and the Strangely Important

edited by Michael Dobson

From the birth of Western civilization to the rescue of Apollo 13, from the Leaning Tower of Pisa to Florence's Duomo, history has often turned on small, improbable details. Whatever happened to the ancient Samaritan people? Why did a fortuitous rainstorm allow the British to conquer India? How did an air raid in Italy lead to the development of chemotherapy? What happened when Albert Einstein met Adolf Hitler on the streets of Berlin? How did the Japanese manage to attack the US mainland using balloons? A cast of award-winning writers tackle some of the strangest tales in history!

US$19.95 print